TOOLS FOR TEACHERS

- **ATOS:** 0.5
- **GRL:** C
- **WORD COUNT:** 39

- **CURRICULUM CONNECTIONS:**
  weather

Skills to Teach

- **HIGH-FREQUENCY WORDS:** are, fun, in, is, it, see, the, they
- **CONTENT WORDS:** arms, cloudy, cold, different, feel, frozen, play, shovel, snowflakes, snows
- **PUNCTUATION:** exclamation points, periods
- **WORD STUDY:** long /e/, spelled *ea* (*each*), spelled *ee* (*see*), spelled *y* (*snowy*); long /o/, spelled *ow* (*snow*); /ow/, spelled *ou* (*cloudy, count*); compound word (*snowflakes*); multisyllable words (*different, frozen*)
- **TEXT TYPE:** explanation

Before Reading Activities

- Read the title and give a simple statement of the main idea.
- Have students "walk" though the book and talk about what they see in the pictures.
- Introduce new vocabulary by having students predict the first letter and locate the word in the text.
- Discuss any unfamiliar concepts that are in the text.

After Reading Activities

Talk to the children about seasons. Do they live in an area that experiences winter? Have they seen snow? If they have, ask the students what they like to do in the snow. If they haven't, have them think of fun activities they would like to do. What kind of clothing would they need? Make a list and discuss the ideas as a group.

Tadpole Books are published by Jump!, 5357 Penn Avenue South, Minneapolis, MN 55419, www.jumplibrary.com

Copyright ©2019 Jump. International copyright reserved in all countries. No part of this book may be reproduced in any form without written permission from the publisher.

Editor: Jenna Trnka   **Designer:** Anna Peterson

Photo Credits: Ariel Skelley/Getty, cover (foreground); LilKar/Shutterstock, cover (background); ronstik/iStock, 1; Milosz_G/Shutterstock, 2–3, 16tm; XiXinXing/iStock, 4–5 (foreground), 14–15, 16bl; trendobjects/iStock, 4–5 (background), 16br; brainmaster/Getty, brainmaster/iStock, Vitalina/iStock, loops7/iStock, 6–7; ChristopherBernard/iStock, 8–9, 16tr; Hayri Er/iStock, 10–11, 16tl; Alexander_Safonov/iStock, 12–13, 16bm.

Library of Congress Cataloging-in-Publication Data
Names: Kenan, Tessa, author.
Title: Snowy / by Tessa Kenan.
Description: Minneapolis, MN : Jump!, Inc., (2018) | Series: Weather report | Includes index.
Identifiers: LCCN 2018005344 (print) | LCCN 2017061691 (ebook) | ISBN 9781641280051 (ebook) | ISBN 9781641280037 (hardcover : alk. paper) | ISBN 9781641280044 (pbk.)
Subjects: LCSH: Snow—Juvenile literature. | Weather—Juvenile literature. Classification: LCC QC926.37 (print) | LCC QC926.37 .K46 2018 (ebook) | DDC 551.57/84—dc23
LC record available at https://lccn.loc.gov/2018005344

SNOWY

by Tessa Kenan

TABLE OF CONTENTS

tadpole books

SNOWY

It is cold.

It is cloudy.

snowflake

It snows!

See the snowflakes.

Each one is different.

Pretty!

They are frozen.

Feel how cold!

arm

Count the arms.

Six.

It snows more.

We shovel.

We play in snow.

It is fun!

WORDS TO KNOW

arms

cloudy

frozen

play

shovel

snowflakes

INDEX